Blessings &
Consecrations

A Book of
Occasional Services

SUPPLEMENTAL WORSHIP RESOURCES 14

ABINGDON PRESS
Nashville

Blessings and Consecrations
A Book of Occasional Services

Copyright © 1984 by Abingdon Press

Second Printing 1984

Library of Congress Cataloging in Publication Data

United Methodist Church (U.S.)
  Blessings and consecrations.
  (Supplemental worship resources; 14)
  1. Occasional services—United Methodist Church
  (U.S.) 2. United Methodist Church (U.S.)—
  Liturgy—Texts. 3. Methodist Church—Liturgy—
  Texts. I. Title. II. Series.
  BX8337.U54   1984   264'.076   83-21541

ISBN 0-687-03626-7

MANUFACTURED BY THE PARTHENON PRESS AT
NASHVILLE, TENNESSEE, UNITED STATES OF AMERICA

The texts of the Sursum Corda, the Sanctus and Benedictus, and the Lord's Prayer are from *Prayers We Have in Common*, copyright © 1970, 1971, and 1975, International Consultation on English Texts. Used by permission.

The chapter beginning on page 23 is reprinted from *An Order of Thanksgiving for the Birth or Adoption of a Child*, copyright © 1980 by the Consultation on Church Union. Used by permission.

The other orders in this book are adapted more or less freely from *The Book of Worship for Church and Home* (Nashville: The United Methodist Publishing House, 1965), as indicated below with BW and page numbers. Other sources from which particular acts of worship are more or less freely adapted are listed below with abbreviations indicated.

The Doctrines and Discipline of the Methodist Episcopal Church and *The Discipline of The Methodist Church. (Discipline 1864 and 1956)*

We Gather Together (Nashville: The United Methodist Publishing House, 1980). *(WGT)*

The Book of Common Prayer. (BCP 1928 or 1977)

The Sacramentary and *The Rites of the Catholic Church* are published in various editions which do not have uniform pagination. *(Sacramentary* and *Rites I* and *II)*

SOURCES OF THE ORDERS

An Order for Organizing a Church. *BW*, 341 ff, *Discipline 1864*, 145, *WGT*, 5 ff, *Sacramentary*.

An Order of Thanksgiving for the Birth or Adoption of a Child. See above.

An Order for Commitment to Christian Service. *BCP 1977*, 420-21.

An Order for the Celebration of an Appointment. *BCP 1977*, 559 ff.

An Order for the Certification of Associates, Directors or Ministers of Education and Associates, Directors or Ministers of Music. *BW*, 334 ff.

An Order for the Recognition of Leaders in the Church. *BW*, 336

An Order for the Recognition of Church-School Workers. *BW*, 337-38.

An Order for the Recognition of Those Engaged in Music Ministries. Original.

An Order for the Breaking of Ground for a Church Building. *BW*, 344 ff, *Discipline 1956*, 618.

An Order for the Laying of a Foundation Stone of a Church Building. *BW*, 348 ff.

An Order for the Consecration of a Church Building. *BW*, 351 ff, *Rites II*, *BCP 1928*, 564-65, *BCP 1977*, 570 ff, *WGT*, 5 ff, *Sacramentary*.

An Order for the Dedication of a Church Building. *BW*, 355 ff, *Rites II*, 222.

An Order for the Consecration of an Educational Building. *BW*, 361 ff.

An Order for the Consecration of a Hospital. *BW*, 365 ff.

An Order for the Consecration of a Dwelling. *BW*, 373-74, *WGT*, 5 ff.

An Order for the Consecration of Church Furnishings and Memorials. *BW*, 372.

An Order for the Dedication of an Organ or Other Musical Instruments. *BW*, 370-71.

Contents

Preface

This book of services for special occasions is the fourteenth in the Supplemental Worship Resources series, developed and sponsored by the Section on Worship of the Board of Discipleship of The United Methodist Church.

When The United Methodist Church was formed in 1968, the hymnals and rituals of both The Evangelical United Brethren and The Methodist Church were retained as the hymnals and Ritual of The United Methodist Church.

It quickly became apparent, however, that there was a need for supplemental worship resources which, while not taking the place of these official resources, would provide alternatives that more fully reflect developments in the contemporary ecumenical church. The General Conference of 1970 authorized the Commission on Worship to begin work on such resources; and the General Conferences of 1972, 1976, and 1980 authorized the Board of Discipleship to continue to provide such resources.

The resulting series of publications began with *The Sacrament of the Lord's Supper: An Alternate Text* (Supplemental Worship Resources 1), which was published in a text edition (1972), a music edition (1975), a Spanish edition (1978), and a revised edition (1981).

Intensive work during the next four years led to the publication in 1976 of *A Service of Baptism, Confirmation, and Renewal* (SWR 2), revised in 1980; *Word and Table: A Basic Pattern of Sunday Worship for United Methodists* (SWR 3), revised in 1980; and *Ritual in a New Day: An Invitation* (SWR 4).

Further work led to the publication in 1979 of *A Service of Christian Marriage* (SWR 5); *Seasons of the Gospel: Resources for the Christian Year* (SWR 6); *A Service of Death and Resurrection* (SWR 7); and *From Ashes to Fire: Services of Worship for the Seasons of Lent and Easter* (SWR 8). *At the Lord's Table: A Communion Service Book for Use by the Minister* (SWR 9) was published in 1981.

The basic general services of the church included in the above publications were revised and collected into *We Gather Together* (SWR 10), which was published in 1980 and commended to local churches for trial use by the 1980 General Conference.

Three hymnals were then prepared. *Songs of Zion* (SWR 12), in the black tradition, was published in 1981; *Supplement to the Book of Hymns* (SWR 11) in 1982; and *Hymns from the Four Winds* (SWR 13), bringing together Asian and Asian-American traditions, in 1983.

There still remained, however, the need to make available to United Methodists in appropriately revised form the "Occasional Offices of the Church" which constitute Part IV of *The Book of Worship for Church and Home*, published by The Methodist Church in 1965.

Blessings and Consecrations is an attempt to meet this need. Like other publications in this series, it represents the corporate work of writers and consultants and of the elected members and staff of the Section on Worship. The Section authorized the preparation of the manuscript and carefully examined the finished manuscript before approving it for publication. Professor Roy Reed of the Methodist Theological Seminary in Ohio was the chief writer, and Dr. Hoyt L. Hickman of the Section staff was editor. Dr. Reed secured the consultative assistance of Cecilia Reed in the writing of the services. The Division of Ordained Ministry of the Board of Higher Education and Ministry was brought into consultation regarding the services pertaining to the ordained ministry that were to be included, and their help in perfecting "An Order for the Celebration of an Appointment" is gratefully acknowledged. The Division of Diaconal Ministry

8

of the same board was brought into consultation regarding the services pertaining to diaconal ministry that were to be included, and their help in perfecting "An Order for the Certification of Associates, Directors or Ministers of Education and Associates, Directors or Ministers of Music" is gratefully acknowledged. The Consultation on Church Union graciously granted permission to use "An Order of Thanksgiving for the Birth or Adoption of a Child." Professor James F. White, formerly of Perkins School of Theology at Southern Methodist University, examined the manuscript and made helpful suggestions. Finally, it will be evident that many of the services are revisions of services in Part IV of *The Book of Worship for Church and Home*, which in many ways is the foundation upon which this book builds.

The members and staff of the Section on Worship, listed below, wish to thank the many persons who have shared with us ideas regarding this book. Reactions and suggestions are welcomed by the Section on Worship, P. O. Box 840, Nashville, Tennessee 37202. We commend this book to the use of the church in the hope that it will be useful in the worship of God and the proclamation of the gospel of Jesus Christ.

Stan DePano, *Chairperson, Section on Worship*
Bishop George W. Bashore
Donald Bueg
Carole Cotton-Winn
D. S. Dharmapalan
Melissa Lynn Ives
J. Sue Kana-Mackey
Merwin Kurtz
Mary Penn
Luis Sotomayor
Sharon Spieth
George W. Watson, Sr.
Langill Watson
Janet Lee, *President, Fellowship of United Methodists in Worship, Music and Other Arts*

Patty Evans, *Executive Secretary-Treasurer, Fellowship of United Methodists in Worship, Music and Other Arts*
Ezra Earl Jones, *General Secretary*
Noé E. Gonzales, *Associate General Secretary*
Hoyt L. Hickman, *Assistant General Secretary and Editor*
Richard L. Eslinger, *Staff*
Barbara P. García, *Staff*
Judy L. Loehr, *Staff*

Introduction

The orders of worship in this collection are for happy occasions. The unique word "bless" means to confer happiness and to hallow or consecrate by religious rite or word. Psalm 65:4 serves well as a prologue to these liturgies:

> Blessed is he whom thou dost
> choose and bring near,
> to dwell in thy courts!
> We shall be satisfied with the goodness
> of thy house,
> thy holy temple!

These orders, which recognize, commission, and bless, are all ceremonies in which persons or things are set apart, usually named, and dedicated to a specific task in the work of Christ's church. Appropriately, the terms "dedicate" and "consecrate" abound in these services. The terms are synonymous. Despite their different roots, the Latin words *consecro* and *dedico* have the same meaning. Likewise, the Greek terms which these Latin words translate have essentially equivalent meanings.

"Dedication" and "consecration" here generally refer to the naming of a special purpose proposed for a person or a thing. When these terms mean or imply the "making sacred" of a person or thing, certain classical theological problems are raised. What it may mean to "make sacred" is a question that has bothered generations of Christians. We may be tempted to ignore the idea of the *consecro*, the "making sacred," and the whole idea of holy existence, in favor of the idea of purpose, stressing dedication as specific action.

This temptation will not be indulged, primarily because there is a close connection made in the New Testament between who a person *is* and what a person *does*. Perhaps the best citation to illustrate this point, in connection with our discussion, is Christ's prayer for the disciples:

Sanctify *[hagiason]* them in the truth; thy word is truth. As thou didst send me into the world, so I have sent them into the world. And for their sake I consecrate *[hagiazo]* myself, that they also may be consecrated *[hagiasmenoi]* in truth. (John 17:17-19)

As the prayer indicates, whoever and whatever is made sacred in this world is made to enter into the consecration of the Christ. This point is made many times in the New Testament. Paul calls Christians into a transforming commitment which he calls the "renewal of your mind" (Romans 12:2). The transformation which he intends is a self-conscious commitment to discover and emulate the "mind" of Christ. It is a call to new being, to existence as a holy and reasonable "living sacrifice" (Romans 12:1). The reality of consecration is, thus, a function of the work of Christ in the world (I John 3:11-24). What a disciple *does* cannot be abstracted from what the disciple *is*.

The Christ who is the "Holy One of God" (Mark 1:24) calls his disciples into his own sanctity through his life and death (John 17:17; Hebrews 13:12; I Peter 1:15; I Corinthians 6:11). The holiness, the *consecro* of Christ, is not an other worldly transcendent essence which can be conveyed through particular "religious experiences" or authorized rites and ceremonies. It is the very power of being which was holy in Christ—not life itself but the *agape* life, which is his gift to us. It is the grace of discipleship which is bestowed upon those who are being made into "a holy temple in the Lord" (Ephesians 2:21) and given the task of a missionary priesthood as a consecrated people (I Peter 2:9).

This consecration and dedication are not enjoined upon some Christians such as ministers or directors of Christian education and withheld from others. All are consecrated and dedicated. The content of the sacrament of baptism proclaims this clearly, and this is reaffirmed in confirmation and other renewals of the baptismal covenant. This is exactly their purpose. Why then, we might ask, do we need *Blessings and Consecrations* to do what has already been done? True, the Spirit is one; insofar as we are consecrated we are all in the one Spirit. But there are many varieties of service; we have different gifts and talents (I Corinthians 12:4-12; Romans 12:4-8).

The purpose of *Blessings and Consecrations* is to recognize some of the varieties in which the one consecration in Christ is realized in the life of the church. The services provided in this collection are not exhaustive of the possibilities for liturgical acts of dedication and consecration. Other liturgies, composed by groups or individuals for special purposes, are possible and desirable. Such services, or "moments" within services, help the Christian community recognize its identity and mission.

It has been pointed out that consecration and dedication are "spiritual" qualities whose essence and meaning cannot be objectified in a liturgical event. This is surely a fact. Many Protestants have pointed to this fact in objection to some of the rites and ceremonies of the church, including sometimes the sacraments, where the subjectivity of the divine presence may seem threatened by the objectifying possibilities inherent in ritual forms of worship. The history of the church demonstrates that such objections are valid. No ceremony properly executed in and of itself alone becomes the guarantor, through ritual words and actions, of the actuality of consecration and dedication. The gifts of Christ, the presence of the Holy Spirit, are not coaxed down by our incantations. In liturgies of blessing we recognize the divine presence, affirm it, and celebrate it; we do not create it. In such ceremonies we may experience together the power of which we speak. The words and actions themselves do not guarantee this experience.

Individual celebrations of the different directions of the one consecration are helpful just because our experience of the one consecration is not uniform, and the variety of our commitments of life in our Lord needs to be articulated and blessed, for our common understanding and enjoyment (blessing).

Such events have their own life; they take place at a given time and in a given place, but only in order that the consecration celebrated can be extended beyond the time-and-place boundaries of a particular service of worship. An individual dedication of a church building, for instance, is not a ceremony in which a secular building is made holy. It is a ceremony where the *one* consecration is recalled as it relates to the life and work of the Christian community that will make its headquarters in this building. The building is dedicated, not that the walls may be magically sacred, or even that a people be sanctified exclusively within the walls, but "for the extension of the kingdom of God."

Such ceremonies are *sacramental* in effect. At the heart of the Holy Communion is the *consecration* where ordinary bread and wine are placed before us and thanks are given for all that God has done, is doing, and will do in Jesus Christ. What takes place is not magic; it is the celebration of the one consecration, which concerns the life of the Christ and his life in us. The bread and wine, the prayers, the action, all are symbols of this one consecration. The dedication of a church building or of a church organ, the blessing of a dwelling, the consecration of church-school workers, are ceremonies of consecration analogous to the consecration in the Lord's Supper. Such services may not be called sacraments, but they are sacramental.

Prior to late medieval theology and the establishing of several liturgical acts as sacraments, many ceremonies were referred to as sacraments. The term had no absolutely fixed reference. After the dogmatizing of sacramental theology in 1439 it became necessary to refer to "occasional" services which were not part of the system of seven sacraments as "sacramentals." Protestants have generally reserved the use of the word "sacrament" for baptism and the Lord's Supper.

The title may be unimportant. What is important is that we relate these acts of consecration and dedication to the one *consecro* in Christ which is the primordial sacrament. Every prayer which consecrates, whether said over bread and wine, church-school workers, church buildings—over any person or thing—is a proclamation of God in Christ, of us in him, and of his rule over the whole created order. Every prayer that blesses and consecrates is a petition that creation should partake of the Lordship of Christ, grow into his likeness and dwell in him.

An Order for Organizing a Church

DECLARATION OF PURPOSE

Dear friends, the Scriptures teach us that the church is the household of God, the body of which Christ is the head, and that it is the design of the gospel to bring together in one all who are in Christ. We have come together to form a new congregation of The United Methodist Church, which is a part of Christ's holy church. Let us dedicate ourselves to this purpose.

HYMN OF PRAISE

OPENING PRAYER

Let us pray.
Lord God, preserve your church. Let your Word be heard and your sacraments lived out among this people, so that they may live in harmony with you and one another, be confirmed in steadfast faith, and be your brave witnesses and workers in the world. **Amen.**

SCRIPTURE LESSON
Jeremiah 32:37-41 or another lesson from the Old Testament

ACT OF PRAISE

For the revelation of yourself which you have given to us through prophets and teachers,
   we praise your name, O Lord.
For salvation from sin through your redeeming love,

we praise your name, O Lord.
For resurrection and new birth in the love of a living Christ,
we praise your name, O Lord.
For the call to discipleship, and the ministry given to all of us in Jesus Christ our Lord,
we praise your name, O Lord.
For the desire of this people to be a congregation in Christ's holy church, and the hope that through them your love will be revealed and demonstrated and your world redeemed,
we praise your name, O Lord,
and pledge ourselves to you this day. Amen.

SCRIPTURE LESSON
II Peter 1:3-10 or another lesson from the New Testament

HYMN

GOSPEL LESSON
Matthew 16:13-18 or another lesson from the Gospels

SERMON

ORGANIZATION OF THE CHURCH
The district superintendent gives opportunity for any to present themselves for membership by certificate of transfer or on profession of faith, receives them according to the ritual of the church, and completes the organization of the church as prescribed in The Book of Discipline.

The district superintendent then says:
By what name shall this church be known?

The pastor or designated lay official answers:
It shall be called the *(Name)* United Methodist Church.

The district superintendent then says:
In accordance with the laws and Discipline of The United Methodist Church, I hereby declare that the *(Name)* United Methodist Church is duly constituted and organized for the glory of God, the proclamation of the gospel, and the service of humanity.

PRAYER

Concerns and prayers, a pastoral prayer, or the following:
Almighty God, whose Son Jesus Christ is the one foundation
and the chief cornerstone of your church: Bless this church
that we have organized in your name. Be the beginning, the
increase, and the consummation of its ministries. Let your
glory be made known in us, and through what we do in your
world. For with the Son and the Holy Spirit you live and
reign, one God, world without end. **Amen.**

*Unless Holy Communion is to be celebrated, the service may
conclude with a hymn and a blessing. If Holy Communion is to be
celebrated, the service continues as follows:*

CONFESSION AND PARDON

Christ our Lord invites to his table all who love him, who
earnestly repent of their sin and seek to live in peace with one
another. Therefore, let us confess our sin before God and one
another.

**Merciful God, we confess that often we have failed to be an
obedient church. We have not done your will, we have
broken your law, we have rebelled against your love, we
have not loved our neighbors, and we have not heard the cry
of the needy. Forgive us, we pray. Free us for joyful
obedience, through Jesus Christ our Lord. Amen.**
All pray in silence.

Minister to people:
Hear the Good News:
Christ died for us while we were yet sinners; that proves
God's love toward us. In the name of Jesus Christ, you are
forgiven!

People to minister:
In the name of Jesus Christ, you are forgiven!

Minister and people:
Glory to God. Amen.

19

THE PEACE

Let us offer one another signs of reconciliation and love.
All exchange signs and words of God's peace.

OFFERING

As forgiven and reconciled people, let us offer ourselves and our gifts to God.

An offering may be received, and a hymn may be sung.

The bread and wine are brought by representatives of the people, or uncovered if already in place.

TAKING THE BREAD AND CUP

The minister takes the bread and cup, and the bread and wine are prepared for the meal.

THE GREAT THANKSGIVING

The Lord be with you.
And also with you.
Lift up your hearts.
We lift them to the Lord.
Let us give thanks to the Lord our God.
It is right to give our thanks and praise.

It is right, and a good and joyful thing, always and everywhere to give thanks to you, Father Almighty, Creator of heaven and earth. You formed us in your image and breathed into us the breath of life. When we turned away, and our love failed, your love remained steadfast. You delivered us from captivity, made covenant to be our sovereign God, and spoke to us through your prophets. And so, with your people on earth and all the company of heaven, we praise your name and join their unending hymn:

Holy, holy, holy Lord, God of power and might,
heaven and earth are full of your glory.
Hosanna in the highest.
Blessed is he who comes in the name of the Lord.
Hosanna in the highest.

Holy are you, and blessed is your Son Jesus Christ. Your Spirit anointed him to preach good news to the poor, to proclaim release to the captives and recovering of sight to the blind, to set at liberty those who are oppressed, and to announce that the time had come when you would save your people. He healed the sick, fed the hungry, and ate with sinners.

By the baptism of his suffering, death, and resurrection you gave birth to your church, delivered us from slavery to sin and death, and made with us a new covenant by water and the Spirit. When the Lord Jesus ascended, he promised to be with us always, in the power of your Word and Holy Spirit.

On the night in which he gave himself up for us he took bread, gave thanks to you, broke the bread, gave it to his disciples, and said: "Take, eat; this is my body which is given for you. Do this in remembrance of me."

When supper was over he took the cup, gave thanks to you, gave it to his disciples, and said: "Drink from this, all of you; this is my blood of the new covenant, poured out for you and for many for the forgiveness of sins. Do this, as often as you drink it, in remembrance of me."

And so, in remembrance of these your mighty acts in Jesus Christ, we offer ourselves in praise and thanksgiving as a holy and living sacrifice, in union with Christ's offering for us, as we proclaim the mystery of faith.

Christ has died, Christ is risen, Christ will come again.

Pour out your Holy Spirit on us, gathered here, and on these gifts of bread and wine. Make them be for us the body and blood of Christ, that we may be for the world the body of Christ, redeemed by his blood.

By your Spirit make us one with Christ, one with each other, and one in ministry to all the world, until Christ comes in final victory and we feast at his heavenly banquet.

21

Through your Son Jesus Christ, with the Holy Spirit in your holy church, all honor and glory is yours, Almighty Father, now and forever. **Amen.**

And now, with the confidence of children of God, let us pray:

**Our Father in heaven, hallowed be your name,
your kingdom come, your will be done,
on earth as in heaven.
Give us today our daily bread.
Forgive us our sins as we forgive those who sin against us.
Save us from the time of trial, and deliver us from evil.
For the kingdom, the power, and the glory are yours,
now and forever. Amen.**

BREAKING THE BREAD

The minister breaks the bread in silence, or while saying:

Because there is one loaf, we, who are many, are one body, for we all partake of the one loaf. The bread which we break is a sharing in the body of Christ.

The minister lifts the cup in silence, or while saying:

The cup over which we give thanks is a sharing in the blood of Christ.

GIVING THE BREAD AND CUP

The bread and wine are given to the people, with these or other words being exchanged:

The body of Christ, given for you. **Amen.**
The blood of Christ, given for you. **Amen.**

The congregation sings hymns while the bread and cup are given. When all have received, the Lord's table is put in order. The following prayer is then offered by the minister or by all:

Most loving God, you have given us a share in the one bread and the one cup and made us one with Christ. Help us to bring your salvation and joy to all the world, in the name of Jesus Christ our Lord. Amen.

HYMN

DISMISSAL WITH BLESSING

Go forth in peace. The grace of the Lord Jesus Christ, and the love of God, and the communion of the Holy Spirit be with you all. **Amen.**

An Order of Thanksgiving for the Birth or Adoption of a Child

This *order* is intended primarily for use within a corporate service of worship. When conducted apart from the fuller liturgical context, appropriate modifications may be made.

One or more of the following Scripture passages may be used in the service of worship:

Deuteronomy 6:4-7
    Diligently teach your children.
Deuteronomy 31:12-13
    "Do . . . this law . . . that their children . . . may hear and learn."
I Samuel 1:9-11, 20-28; 2:26
    The birth and presentation of Samuel.
Psalm 8
    "O Lord, our Lord, how majestic is your name in all the earth!"
Psalm 78:1-7
    Tell to the coming generations the glorious deeds of the Lord.
Matthew 18:1-4
    Those who humble themselves like children will be greatest.
Mark 10:13-16
    Jesus blesses the children.

Luke 2:22-32, 52
The presentation of Jesus in the temple.

PRESENTATION

Members of Christ's family, I present to you *(Name)* and *(Name)* together with *(Name)* whose coming into their home they now acknowledge with gratitude and faith.

CALL TO THANKSGIVING

Within the family of Christ, the birth or adoption of a child is an occasion for thanksgiving. Life is God's gift, and children are a heritage from the Lord. Therefore we who are entrusted with their care are given both great responsibility and opportunity. Because God has favored us through the coming of this child, let us offer our praise.

HYMN OF PRAISE, PSALM, OR CANTICLE

PRAYER

For the birth of a child, the following or another prayer is offered.
O God, like a mother who comforts her children, you strengthen us in our solitude, sustain and provide for us. We come before you with gratitude for the gift of this child, for the joy which has come into this family, and the grace with which you surround them and all of us. As a father cares for his children, so continually look upon us with compassion and goodness. Pour out your Spirit. Enable your servants to abound in love,
and establish our homes in holiness; through Jesus Christ our Lord. **Amen.**

For the adoption of a child, the following or another prayer is offered.
O God, you have adopted all of us as your children. We give thanks to you for the child who has come to bless this family and for the parents who have welcomed this child as their own. By the power of your Holy Spirit, fill their home with love, trust, and understanding; through Jesus Christ our Lord. **Amen.**

NAMING OF THE CHILD

Minister: What name have you given this child?
Those presenting the child respond.
   However, *if the name is to be conferred as part of this order, the minister instead asks:*
   What name do you now give this child?
   Those presenting the child may place their hands upon the child. They respond:
   We name you *(Name)*.

THE THANKSGIVING

Minister to family: In accepting *(Name)* as a gift from God, you also acknowledge your faith in Jesus Christ and the responsibility which God places upon you.

The members of the family respond saying or repeating after the minister:
We receive *(Name)*
from the hand of a loving Creator.
With humility and hope
we accept the obligation which is ours
to love and nurture *(her/him)*
and to lead *(her/him)* to Christian faith
by our teaching and example.
We ask for the power of the Holy Spirit
and the support of the church
that we may be good stewards
of this gift of life.

Minister to congregation: The church is the family of Christ, the community in which we grow in faith and commitment.

Congregation:
We rejoice to take *(Name)* under our care. We seek God's grace to be a community in which the gospel is truly proclaimed to all. We will support you and minister with you as workers together in Christ Jesus and heirs of his promise.

25

The minister takes the child and says:
(Name), may the eternal God bless you and watch over you.
May Jesus Christ incorporate you into his death and
resurrection through baptism.

(If the child has previously been baptized, delete "through
baptism.")

May the Holy Spirit sanctify you and bring you to life
everlasting.
The minister returns the child to the family.

PRAYER

Gracious God, from whom every family in heaven and on
earth is named: out of the treasures of your glory strengthen
us through your Spirit. Help us joyfully to nurture *(Name)*
within your church. Bring *(her/him)* to baptism (or to
Christian maturity), that Christ may dwell in *(her/his)* heart
through faith. Give power to *(Name)* and to us, that with all
your people we may grasp the breadth and length, the height
and depth of Christ's love. Enable us to know this love,
though it is beyond knowledge, and to be filled with your
own fullness; through Jesus Christ our Lord. Amen.

*If the Lord's Prayer is not used at another point in the service, it may
be prayed by all here.*

ASCRIPTION

Glory to God, who by the power at work among us is able to
do far more than we can ask or imagine. Glory be given to this
God from generation to generation in the church and in
Christ Jesus forever! **Amen.**

An Order for Commitment to Christian Service

This *order* is intended to recognize and consecrate a
commitment to the service of Christ in the world, either in

general terms or in connection with a particular responsibility in the world or in the church.

Renewal of the baptismal covenant may be used as an alternative to this form, since baptism is every Christian's ordaining sacrament and its renewal is appropriate to celebrate any form of commitment to Christian service. See *A Service of Baptism, Confirmation, and Renewal.*

As a response to the Word or at some other appropriate place within a public worship service, the minister meets the person or persons undertaking some special responsibility before the Lord's table and says:

Dear friends, today we recognize the ministry of *(Name(s))* and consecrate *(her, him, each of them)* to a special task in the service of Jesus Christ.

The minister then says whatever is appropriate concerning the form of service and the person(s) being consecrated.

(Name), in the name of this congregation I commend you to this work and pledge you our prayers, encouragement, and support. May the Holy Spirit guide and strengthen you, that in this, and in all things you may do God's will in the service of Jesus Christ.

Let us pray.
Almighty God, look with favor upon *this person* who reaffirms commitment to follow Christ and to serve in his name. Give *(her, him, each of them)* courage, patience, and vision; and strengthen us all in our Christian vocation of witness to the world and of service to others; through Jesus Christ our Lord. **Amen.**

Other prayers may be added.

The order for commitment may conclude with the exchange of the peace of Christ.

An Order for the Celebration of an Appointment

This *order* is intended for use by a congregation whose minister has been newly appointed or reappointed according to the polity of The United Methodist Church, although with appropriate adaptations it could be used by congregations of other denominations as well. It is intended primarily for use within a corporate service of worship. It may be led by the chairperson of the Pastor-Parish Relations Committee or by some other designated leader in the congregation.

Before the reading of the Scripture lessons, the minister comes before the Lord's table and the person officiating says to the congregation:

Dear friends, today we welcome *(Name)*, who has been (re)appointed to serve as minister of *(name of church)*.

We believe that *(she/he)* is well qualified and has been prayerfully and wisely appointed.

The person officiating then says to the minister:
(Name), you have committed yourself to live among us as a bearer of the Word of God; minister of the sacraments; and sustainer of the love, order, and discipleship of the people of God.

The minister responds:
Today I reaffirm this commitment in the presence of this congregation.

The person officiating says to the congregation:
Brothers and sisters in Christ, as a people committed to participate in the ministries of the church by your prayers, your presence, your gifts, and your service, will you who celebrate this new beginning support and uphold *(Name)* in these ministries?

The congregation responds:
we have committed ourselves, and we reaffirm our commitment.

The person officiating continues:
Let us pray.
Eternal God, strengthen and sustain us in our ministries together, with *(Name)* as our pastor. Give *(her/him)* and us patience, courage, and wisdom so to care for one another and challenge one another that together we may follow Jesus Christ, living together in love, and offering our gifts and talents in your service, through Jesus Christ our Lord. **Amen.**

As the minister stands at the Lord's table, several people come forward to make presentations. As these are received, the minister places them on the table. Other presentations may be made and some of those here omitted, as deemed appropriate.

Presenter: (Name), accept this Bible,
and be among us as one who proclaims the Word.
Minister: **Amen.**

Presenter: (Name), take this water,
and baptize new Christians in this place.
Minister: **Amen.**

Presenter: (Name), take this bread and cup,
and keep us in communion with Christ and his church.
Minister: **Amen.**

Presenter: (Name), receive this hymnal,
and guide us in our prayer and praise.
Minister: **Amen.**

Presenter: (Name), receive this stole,
and shepherd us as a pastor.
Minister: **Amen.**

Presenter: (Name), receive this *Book of Discipline,*
and strengthen our connections as United Methodists.
Minister: **Amen.**

Presenter: (Name), receive this globe,
and lead us in our mission to the community and the world.
Minister: **Amen.**

Minister: Let us pray.

Congregation and minister: **Lord God, bless the ministries of your church. We thank you for the variety of gifts you have bestowed upon us. Draw us together in one Spirit, that each of us may use our differing gifts as members of one body. May your Word be proclaimed with faithfulness, and may we be doers of your Word and not hearers only. As we who have died and risen with Christ in baptism gather at his table and then scatter into the world, may we be one in service to others, in the name of Jesus Christ our Lord. Amen.**

Minister: The peace of the Lord be always with you.
Congregation: **And also with you.**

An Order for the Certification of Associates, Directors or Ministers of Education and Associates, Directors or Ministers of Music

This *order* may be used to certify associates, directors, or ministers of education and associates, directors, or ministers of music at Annual Conference at the time of the report of the Conference Board of Diaconal Ministry. Presiders may be the bishop, district superintendent, or chairperson of the Conference Board of Diaconal Ministry.

OPENING PRAYER

Blessed are you, O Lord God,
from this time forth and for evermore!
With my whole heart I seek you;
your service is my light and life.

DECLARATION OF PURPOSE

For associate, director, or minister of education:

Dear friends, we acknowledge that the teaching of believers is a gift of the Holy Spirit, and we affirm the call to this ministry. We desire to be taught the truth of God's ways in faithful discipleship to Jesus, our Teacher.

For associate, director, or minister of music:
Dear friends, we acknowledge that the offering of music is a gift of the Holy Spirit, and we affirm the call to this ministry. We affirm its place of blessing in our prayer and praise, both in the house of God and in our unceasing worship.

PRESENTATION

A designated member of the Conference Board of Diaconal Ministry brings forward those who are to be recognized, and says:

Bishop and members of this conference, I present to you *(Names)*, who are seeking certification as associate, director, or minister of education, or associate, director, or minister of music. *These persons* have fulfilled the professional requirements of The United Methodist Church for this certification, have demonstrated *their* call to this particular ministry, and desire to be so recognized.

The above may be repeated for each category of certification.

THE COMMITMENT

Sisters and brothers, by the grace of God, we desire to recognize *these persons* as *(category of certification)* in The United Methodist Church. Do you affirm *these persons* in their call to this special ministry and support their desire to serve?

We affirm these persons in their call and are willing to support their special ministry.

To those who are to be certified:

Do you believe in your heart that you have been led by the Spirit of God to assume the responsibilities of the work in which you are to be certified?

I do so believe.

Will you strive to live so that the power of God may be manifest in your life and ministry, enabling you to bring others to an awareness of the presence of God and to continue as disciples of our Lord Jesus Christ?

I will, by God's grace.

For associate, director, or minister of education:
Will you accept the duties which have been committed to your care, encouraging in the church the desire for knowledge and wisdom in the ways of God by administering and participating in the teaching ministry?

For associate, director, or minister of music:
Will you accept the duties which have been committed to your care, encouraging in the church the liveliness of worship, music, and all the arts in their various forms?

And will you do this faithfully, to the glory of God and in the service of the people of God?

I will do so, the Lord being my helper.

THE CERTIFICATION

The presider, taking the right hand of each person to be recognized, says:

(Name), be enabled by the grace of God to fulfill the responsibility of *(category of certification)* in the church. In the name of the Father, the Son, and the Holy Spirit. **Amen.**

CLOSING PRAYER

Almighty God, look with favor on these your servants who are recognized this day in the call to the ministry of *(education, music)*. Grant that they may have strength of body, mind, and spirit for the fulfillment of your will, that they may worthily discharge the ministry committed to them to the blessing of your people and the glory of Jesus Christ, our Lord and Savior. **Amen.**

An Order for the Recognition of Leaders in the Church

This *order* may be included in a service of worship when elected or appointed leaders in the church are to be installed or recognized.

Dear friends, you have been called by God and chosen by the people of God for leadership in the church. This ministry is a blessing and a serious responsibility. It recognizes your special gifts and calls you to work among us and for us. In love we thank you for accepting your obligation and challenge you to offer your best to the Lord, to this people, and to our ministry in the world. Live a life in Christ and make him known in your witness and your work.

Today we recognize *(Names)*.

Do you this day acknowledge yourself a faithful disciple of Jesus Christ?

I do.

Will you devote yourself to the service of God in the world?

I will.

Will you so live that you enable this church to be a people of love and peace?

I will.

Will you do all in your power to be responsible to the task for which you have been chosen?

I will.

Let us pray.
Almighty God, pour out your blessings upon these your servants who have been given particular ministries in your church. Grant them grace to give themselves wholeheartedly in your service. Keep before them the example of our Lord,

who thought not first of himself, but gave himself for us all. Let them share his ministry and consecration, that they may enter into his joy. Guide them in their work. Reward their faithfulness with the knowledge that through them your purposes are accomplished through Jesus Christ our Lord. **Amen.**

Dear friends, rejoice that God provides laborers for the vineyards. Do all you can to assist and encourage them in these responsibilities to which they have been called, giving them your cooperation, your counsel, and your prayers.

The minister may greet the leaders individually.

A hymn may be sung and a blessing given.

An Order for the Recognition of Church-School Workers

This *order* may be included in a service of worship when church-school workers are to be installed or recognized.

Dear friends, let us recognize those who have responded to the call of God to become workers in the church school. To teach, to administer the work of teaching, and to support the work of teaching are ministries of Christ among us. Those called to these ministries need our loyal support and our prayers.

The chairperson of education or the minister reads the names of the persons to be recognized, and they come forward to stand before the minister, who says to them:

Friends and co-workers, the ministry of teaching in the church is a gift. In the body of Christ this gift is shared among many whom God appoints to instruct us all in faith and holiness. Those who teach are also called to be learners.

"Teach me, O Lord, the way of your statutes; and I will keep it to the end. Give me understanding, that I may keep your law and observe it with my whole heart" (Psalms 119:33-34).

Like Jesus, in the temple as a youth, they and those they teach will listen to the Word of God and ask questions.

"Through your precepts I get understanding; therefore I hate every false way. Your word is a lamp to my feet and a light to my path" (Psalm 119:104-105).

Like Jesus, they will teach with authority the truth about our God of justice and mercy.

"For ever, O Lord, your word is firmly fixed in the heavens. Your faithfulness endures to all generations; you have established the earth, and it stands fast" (Psalm 119:89-90).

Like Jesus, they will tell of God in stories and parables, making their witness in God's continuing story.

"Your testimonies are wonderful; therefore my soul keeps them. The unfolding of your words gives light; it imparts understanding to the simple" (Psalm 119:129-30).

Like Jesus, they will seek God in prayer, and from Jesus they will learn to bless the hallowed name and seek the eternal kingdom.

"Let my cry come before you, O Lord; give me understanding according to your word! Let my prayer come before you; deliver me according to your word" (Psalm 119:169-70).

The minister then leads the congregation in this prayer:
Let us pray.
O God, you sent your beloved Son to be to us the way, the truth, and the life. Give your blessing, and the guidance of your Holy Spirit, to these your servants, and to us all, that we may teach faithfully, nurture your children, increase your kingdom, and glorify your name, through Jesus Christ our Lord. **Amen.**

The minister may greet the church-school workers individually. A hymn may be sung and a blessing given.

An Order for the Recognition of Those Engaged in Music Ministries

This *order* may be included in a service of worship when choirs, their directors, and instrumentalists are to be installed or recognized.

Dear friends, let us recognize those who have responded to the call of God to the ministry of music in the church. To direct, to sing, and to play instruments are ministries of Christ among us. Those called to these ministries need our loyal support and our prayers.

The chairperson of worship or the minister reads the names of the persons to be recognized, and they come forward to stand before the minister, who says to them:

Making music to the praise of God in the congregation is a ministry which requires devotion and discipline. Are you ready to accept responsibility for this ministry?

I am.

Will you be faithful to the disciplines of music?

I will.

May the faith which your music expresses live in your heart; and what you believe in your heart, practice in your life. And may God give you grace to offer your music and your life in faithfulness and consecration, now, and in the world to come.

The minister then leads the congregation in this prayer:
O Lord, our God, bless these ministries of music and those who offer them in your service. Grant, we pray, to these

persons love for you and your people, fullness of heart as they praise you, and diligence that their music may be a worthy offering to your glory, through Jesus Christ our Lord. **Amen.**

The minister then says to the congregation:

Dear friends, I commend to you these persons. To them has been given the ministry of music in the church. Sustain them with your encouragement and your prayers, as together we seek to offer praise to God.

The minister may greet the persons individually. A hymn may be sung and a blessing given.

An Order for the Breaking of Ground for a Church Building

This *order* is designed to be a service of worship in itself.

The people may assemble at the construction site, or they may gather in a suitable place and process to the site. If the people process to the site following a service in their present house of worship, this *order* may begin at the site with the breaking of ground.

A wooden cross may be erected at the place where the Lord's table will be located, if this is appropriate to the condition of the construction site.

The use of banners and colorful vestments can add to the joyful, festive character of the celebration.

SCRIPTURE SENTENCES

Give to the Lord the glory due to his name;
bring an offering,
and come into his courts.

Praise waits for you, O God,
and to you shall the vow be performed.

Our help is in the name of the Lord,
who made heaven and earth.

**Except the Lord build the house
they labor in vain that build it.**

HYMN OF PRAISE

OPENING PRAYER

Let us pray.
Almighty and everlasting God, ever exalted yet always near:
be present with us, gathered together here to set apart this
ground upon which we stand to the honor and glory of your
great name. Let your Spirit descend upon your church which
will come together here, and within these walls let your glory
dwell. Fill with your love all who shall seek your face here;
and as they depart from this place, go with them in the peace
and power of your Holy Spirit; through Jesus Chrst our Lord.
Amen.

SCRIPTURE LESSON—*I Chronicles 21:28–22:16*
            or Genesis 28:11-18

ACT OF PRAISE—*Psalm 122:1-2, 6-9*
            or Psalm 87, with *II Chronicles 7:16* as a
            refrain—"I have chosen and sanctified
            this place."

SCRIPTURE LESSON—*Ephesians 4:1-7, 11-13*

ANTHEM OR HYMN

GOSPEL LESSON—*John 4:19-24*

SERMON

BREAKING OF GROUND

To the glory of God, in the presence of this congregation, I
now direct that ground be broken for the *(Name)* United
Methodist Church. The responsibility and the privilege rests

upon us to cause a building to rise here which shall be a house of this people of God and a place devoted to the worship of Almighty God and to the glory of his blessed Son, our Lord and Savior Jesus Christ.

As each one of those selected turns a spadeful of earth, the minister says one of the following sentences, to which the people respond:

That a church may meet here where children shall learn to love God and grow in grace and goodness, and in favor with God and all people,

we break this ground today.

That a church may meet here where youth shall be inspired to pause to pray and rise to serve,

we break this ground today.

That a church may meet here where the weary and heavy-laden shall find inner peace which the world can neither give nor take away,

we break this ground today.

That a church may meet here where the Word of God shall be so read and preached that it shall become the Living Word, and the sacraments so celebrated that all life shall become sacramental,

we break this ground today.

That a church may meet here where multitudes shall be refreshed in spirit, relieved from pain, released from bondage, and redeemed from sin,

we break this ground today.

That a church may meet here where the grace of God may make our human lives into a Christlike love and our homes places of living witness for that kingdom where Christ is Lord,

we break this ground today.

That a church may rise here from which, by the power of the Holy Spirit, your people are sent forth into this community and all the world as champions of justice and love to all people,

we break this ground today.

Other sentences and responses may be added.

CLOSING PRAYER

Let us pray.

Lord God, you fill the whole world with your presence, that your name may be hallowed everywhere. Bless us who meet here, on this ground made holy by your worship. Consecrate those whose vision and work provide this site. Help us to rejoice in this work just begun and to persevere to its completion, so that this place may resound with your praises and become for us a home where we may together be nurtured in the faith of our Lord Jesus Christ. **Amen.**

THE LORD'S PRAYER

HYMN

BLESSING

An Order for the Laying of a Foundation Stone of a Church Building

This *order* is designed to be a service of worship in itself.

The people may assemble at the site of the new building, or they may gather in a suitable place and process to the site. If the people process to the site following a service in their present house of worship, this *order* may begin at the site with the laying of the foundation stone.

SCRIPTURE SENTENCES

Our help is in the name of the Lord,
who made heaven and earth.
Unless the Lord builds the house,
those who build it labor in vain.

HYMN OF PRAISE: "The Church's One Foundation"

DECLARATION OF PURPOSE

Friends, we are assembled to lay the foundation stone of a new house of worship. Let us faithfully and devoutly seek the blessing of God on what we do.

OPENING PRAYER

Let us pray.
Almighty and everlasting God, exalted yet near, we offer to you this foundation for a house of praise and prayer where your glory shall be manifest among us, and from which your people shall go forth in ministry to all the world; through Jesus Christ our Lord. **Amen.**

SCRIPTURE LESSON—*Isaiah 28:16-17*

ACT OF PRAISE—*Psalm 24 (read responsively or sung)*

SCRIPTURE LESSON—*Ephesians 2:19-22*

ANTHEM OR HYMN

GOSPEL LESSON—*Matthew 7:24-27*

SERMON

LAYING OF THE FOUNDATION STONE

If items are to be placed in the foundation stone they should be brought forward at this time and displayed before the people. These may include a Bible, hymnal, Book of Discipline, *appropriate names and pictures, and other things suitable. When these have been placed in a box and put in the foundation stone the minister stands at the side of the stone and says:*

"According to the grace of God given to me, like a skilled master builder I laid a foundation. . . . For no other foundation can any one lay than that which is laid, which is Jesus Christ" (I Corinthians 3:10*a*, 11).

Then with the aid of the builder or other persons chosen, the stone is put in place.

Praise the Lord,
because the foundation of the house of the Lord is laid!

Praise the Lord. Hallelujah!

CLOSING PRAYERS

Then the minister, hand placed upon the stone, continues:

Let us pray.
Almighty God, on whom we build all our hopes, with your loving-kindness bless this place where we lay the foundation of a house to the praise and honor of your holy name. Accept the act by which we lay this foundation stone. Bless those whose offerings enable us to build this house. Guard and direct those who labor in building it, shielding them from accident and peril. May the walls of this building rise in security and in beauty; and may the hearts of these your people be fitly joined together into a living temple, built upon the foundation of the apostles and prophets, Jesus Christ being the chief cornerstone. **Amen.**

THE LORD'S PRAYER

HYMN

BLESSING

An Order for the Consecration of a Church Building

This *order* is based on the ancient tradition that the consecration of a church building is the proclamation of the

Word and the celebration of the Holy Communion as the first act of worship in the new building.

It is appropriate and also an ancient tradition that the congregation and leaders of worship gather at some place outside the building and enter in procession for the consecration service.

Before the procession the people may read or sing Psalm 24.

Certain things which will be used in worship may be carried in the procession, such as a Bible, water for the baptismal font, vessels for the Communion bread and wine, a cross, hangings for the Lord's table, and other works of art. Hymns may be sung in the procession. If the choir leads the procession, it may assemble in the church and sing anthems as the people enter.

DECLARATION OF PURPOSE

Brothers and sisters in Christ, this is a day of rejoicing. We have come together to consecrate this building of *(Name)* United Methodist Church. Let us open our hearts and minds to receive God's Word with faith. May our blessed communion, born of one baptism and nurtured at one table of the Lord, become one temple of the Holy Spirit as we gather in love.

PRESENTATION OF THE BUILDING

A person or persons designated come forward and say(s):

(I, we) present this building to be consecrated to the glory of God and the service of all people.

NAMING OF THE BUILDING

Bishop, district superintendent, or their representative:

By what name shall this house be known?

Pastor or designated lay official:
It shall be called the *(Name)* United Methodist Church.

CONSECRATION OF THE BUILDING

Dear friends, rejoice that God so moved the hearts of people that this house has been built for praise and prayer. Let us now consecrate it for service and celebrate its holy use.

Several persons may lead sections of the following prayer of consecration, which the officiating minister should begin and conclude.

Let us pray.
O eternal God, mighty in power and of incomprehensible majesty, whom the heavens cannot contain, much less the walls of temples made with hands. You have promised your special presence whenever two or three are assembled in your name to offer praise and prayer.

By the power of your Holy Spirit consecrate this house of your worship. Bless us and sanctify what we do here, that this place may be holy for us and a house of prayer for all people.

Guide and empower in this place by the same Spirit the proclamation of your Word and the celebration of your sacraments, the pouring out of prayer and the singing of your praise, professions of faith and testimonies to your grace, the joining of men and women in marriage and the celebration of death and resurrection.

Save us from that failure of vision which would confine our worship within these walls, but send us out from here to be your servants in the world, sharing the blessings of Christ with the world he came to redeem.

The officiating minister concludes:
Now, O God, Father, Son, and Holy Spirit: sanctify this place, for everything in heaven and on earth is yours. Yours, Lord, is the kingdom, and you are exalted as head above all. **Amen.**

HYMN OR ANTHEM

CONSECRATION OF THE PULPIT
Those leading in worship process to the pulpit.
The officiating minister lays a hand upon the pulpit and says:

Let us pray.

Eternal God, we thank you that Christ your living Word speaks to us through the words of Holy Scripture, written of old by the inspiration of your Holy Spirit and proclaimed today by the anointing of the same Spirit.

When your Word is read and preached from this pulpit, purify the lives and lips of those who speak here, that your Word alone may be proclaimed and your Word alone may be heard and obeyed. May the words of our mouths and the meditations of our hearts be acceptable to you, our Rock and our Redeemer, through Jesus Christ our Lord. **Amen.**

God's Word is a lantern to our feet and a light upon our path. We consecrate this pulpit in the name of the Father, and of the Son, and of the Holy Spirit. **Amen.**

A Bible is placed upon the pulpit at this time.

SCRIPTURE LESSON—*I Kings 8:22-30 or Genesis 28:11-18*

ACT OF PRAISE—*Psalm 122:1-2, 6-9,* with *I Chronicles 7:16* as a refrain—"I have chosen and sanctified this place."

SCRIPTURE LESSON—*I Corinthians 3:9b-13, 16-17 or Revelation 21:2-7, 22-25 or Hebrews 10:19-25*

HYMN

GOSPEL LESSON—*Matthew 16:13-18 or Matthew 21:10-14*

SERMON

HYMN OF INVITATION OR RESPONSE

CONSECRATION OF THE BAPTISMAL FONT
Those leading in worship process to the baptismal font.
The officiating minister lays a hand upon the font and says:

Let us pray.
Most gracious God, we thank you that through the waters of baptism you have given us new life, adopted us as your children, and made us members of your church.

When we pour the water of baptism, making and renewing our covenant vows, pour out your Spirit and give new birth; wash away sin and clothe your people in righteousness; that, dying and being raised with Christ, we may walk in new and abundant life; through the same Jesus Christ our Lord. **Amen.**

There is one Lord, one faith, one baptism, one God and Father of us all. We consecrate this font in the name of the Father, and of the Son, and of the Holy Spirit. **Amen.**

Water is poured into the font at this time. Persons may be baptized.

CONSECRATION OF THE LORD'S TABLE

Those leading in worship process to the Lord's table.
The officiating minister lays a hand upon the table and says:

Let us pray.
Lord God, We thank you that when we gather at the Lord's table the living Christ is known to us in the breaking of the bread and the sharing of the cup, and we are renewed as his body, whose life is in his blood. When we eat this bread and drink from this cup, refresh all those who partake at this holy table. Feed the hunger of our hearts with the bread of heaven, and quench our deepest thirst with the cup of salvation. Strengthen us for your service in the world, and give us a foretaste of the feast to come, through Jesus Christ our Lord. **Amen.**

Jesus said, "Whoever comes to me shall not hunger, and whoever believes in me shall never thirst." We consecrate this table in the name of the Father, and of the Son, and of the Holy Spirit. **Amen.**

An offering may be received.

A hymn may be sung while the gifts are brought to the Lord's table.

Communion vessels, bread, and wine are placed upon the table at this time. Flowers may be placed near the table, and candles may be lit.

TAKING THE BREAD AND CUP

The minister takes the bread and cup, and the bread and wine are prepared for the meal.

THE GREAT THANKSGIVING

The Lord be with you.
And also with you.
Lift up your hearts.
We lift them to the Lord.
Let us give thanks to the Lord our God.
It is right to give our thanks and praise.
It is right, and a good and joyful thing, always and everywhere to give thanks to you, Father Almighty, Creator of heaven and earth. You formed us in your image and breathed into us the breath of life. When we turned away, and our love failed, your love remained steadfast. You delivered us from captivity, made covenant to be our sovereign God, and spoke to us through your prophets. And so, with your people on earth and all the company of heaven, we praise your name and join their unending hymn:

Holy, holy, holy Lord, God of power and might, heaven and earth are full of your glory. Hosanna in the highest. Blessed is he who comes in the name of the Lord. Hosanna in the highest.

Holy are you, and blessed is your Son Jesus Christ. Your Spirit anointed him to preach good news to the poor, to proclaim release to the captives and recovering of sight to the blind, to set at liberty those who are oppressed, and to announce that the time had come when you would save your people. He healed the sick, fed the hungry, and ate with sinners.

By the baptism of his suffering, death, and resurrection you gave birth to your church, delivered us from slavery to sin and death, and made with us a new covenant by water and the Spirit. When the Lord Jesus ascended, he promised to

47

be with us always, in the power of your Word and Holy Spirit.

On the night in which he gave himself up for us he took bread, gave thanks to you, broke the bread, gave it to his disciples, and said: "Take, eat; this is my body which is given for you. Do this in remembrance of me."

When supper was over he took the cup, gave thanks to you, gave it to his discples, and said: "Drink from this, all of you; this is my blood of the new covenant, poured out for you and for many for the forgiveness of sins. Do this, as often as you drink it, in remembrance of me."

And so, in remembrance of these your mighty acts in Jesus Christ, we offer ourselves in praise and thanksgiving as a holy and living sacrifice, in union with Christ's offering for us, as we proclaim the mystery of faith.

Christ has died, Christ is risen, Christ will come again.

Pour out your Holy Spirit on us, gathered here, and on these gifts of bread and wine. Make them be for us the body and blood of Christ, that we may be for the world the body of Christ, redeemed by his blood.

By your Spirit make us one with Christ, one with each other, and one in minstry to all the world, until Christ comes in final victory and we feast at his heavenly banquet.

Through your Son Jesus Christ, with the Holy Spirit in your holy church, all honor and glory is yours, Almighty Father, now and forever.

Amen.

And now, with the confidence of children of God, let us pray:

**Our Father in heaven, hallowed be your name,
your kingdom come, your will be done,
on earth as in heaven.
Give us today our daily bread.**

Forgive us our sins as we forgive those who sin against us. Save us from the time of trial, and deliver us from evil. For the kingdom, the power, and the glory are yours, now and forever. Amen.

BREAKING THE BREAD

The minister breaks the bread in silence, or while saying:

Because there is one loaf, we, who are many, are one body, for we all partake of the one loaf. The bread which we break is a sharing in the body of Christ.

The minister lifts the cup in silence, or while saying:
The cup over which we give thanks is a sharing in the blood of Christ.

GIVING THE BREAD AND CUP

The bread and wine are given to the people, with these or other words being exchanged:

The body of Christ, given for you. **Amen.**
The blood of Christ, given for you. **Amen.**

The congregation sings hymns while the bread and cup are given. When all have received, the Lord's table is put in order.

The following prayer is then offered by the minister or by all:

Most loving God, you have given us a share in the one bread and the one cup and made us one with Christ. Help us bring your salvation and joy to all the world, in the name of Jesus Christ our Lord. Amen.

HYMN

DISMISSAL WITH BLESSING

Go forth in peace. The grace of the Lord Jesus Christ, and the love of God, and the communion of the Holy Spirit be with you all. **Amen.**

An Order for the Dedication of a Church Building

This *order* is designed to be a service of worship in itself. It may be used for the dedication of a church sanctuary, a school building, or a parish house.

The 1945 edition of *The Book of Worship* of The Methodist Church made the first distinction between the dedication of a church building and the consecration or opening of a church for worship. The basis for this difference is the provision in the *Discipline* of the uniting church (1939) that "before any church building may be formally dedicated it shall be necessary to discharge all indebtedness against it" (¶784). The need for a ceremony to open and use a building for the first time was soon felt, and such a ceremony appeared in the *Discipline* of 1944 (¶1930) and in *The Book of Worship* (1945). In *The Book of Worship* (1965) the word "consecrating" was added to the title, establishing a distinction between consecrating and dedicating a church building (p. 351). For more historical information concerning these orders, see *Companion to the Book of Worship*, William F. Dunkle, Jr., and Joseph D. Quillian, Jr., eds. (Abingdon Press, 1970), pp. 202ff.

"An Order for the Dedication of a Church Building" below suggests that a ceremony of mortgage-burning may be included. What is actually burned ought to be a *copy* of the mortgage and not the original mortgage itself, which should be preserved. In some communities, fire codes may require that the service or part of it be held outdoors. This might include a processional where the service begins in the church building and moves outdoors for the mortgage-burning. In any event, a procession is appropriate and might include the bringing forward of the document to be burned, a vessel in which the burning will take place (a large bowl should suffice), and all the persons who will be involved in the service.

Since a mortgage-burning is a climax of something begun in the past, it is a good time to dedicate something which indicates the congregation's hope and its future, or to inaugurate new programs.

In the burning ceremony itself the copy of the mortgage might be presented to the pastor or district superintendent by one of the trustees. The burning can be accompanied by an anthem of praise, or a brief witness to the congregation by several representatives of the different ministries of the church—such as worship, education, evangelism, mission—concerning the meaning of this event and hopes for the future; or the burning could take place concurrent with an appropriate reading such as Psalm 24, punctuated by phrases from the prayer of Solomon in I Kings 8:27-30.

CALL TO PRAISE

It is good to give thanks to the Lord,
to sing praises to your name, O Most High;
to declare your steadfast love in the morning
and your faithfullness by night.
Bless our God, O peoples,
let the sound of his praise be heard.
My lips will shout for joy,
when I sing praises to you;
my soul also which you rescued.

HYMN OF PRAISE

OPENING PRAYER

Let us pray.
Eternal God, let this building, which we dedicate to your name, be a house of salvation and grace where Christians gathered together may learn of you, may worship you in spirit and truth, and grow together in love. Grant this through Christ our Lord. **Amen.**

ANTHEM OR HYMN

SCRIPTURE LESSON—*Isaiah 55:6-13 or I Kings 8:22-30*
or Jeremiah 31:31-34

51

ACT OF PRAISE—*Psalm 24, read responsively or sung*

SCRIPTURE LESSON—*Ephesians 2:19-22*
  or Revelation 21:2-7, 22-25 or I Corinthians 3:9b-13, 16-17

HYMN

GOSPEL LESSON—*Matthew 16:13-18 or Matthew 21:10-14*
                or Matthew 7:24-27

SERMON

BURNING OF THE MORTGAGE

OFFERING

ACT OF DEDICATION

Any sections below which do not apply to the functions of the building being dedicated may be omitted.

Dear friends, let us dedicate this building and rejoice in its holy use. To the glory of God the Father, who has called us by grace; to the honor of his Son, who loved us and gave himself for us; to the praise of the Holy Spirit, who illumines and sanctifies us;

we dedicate this house.

For the worship of God in prayer and praise;
for the preaching of the everlasting gospel;
for the celebration of the holy sacraments;

we dedicate this house.

For the comfort of all who mourn;
for strength to those who are tempted;
for light to those who seek the way;

we dedicate this house.

For the hallowing of family life;
for teaching and guiding the young;
for the perfecting of the saints;

we dedicate this house.

For the conversion of sinners;
for the promotion of righteousness;
for the extension of the kingdom of God;

we dedicate this house.

In the unity of the faith;
in the bond of brotherhood and sisterhood;
in love and good will to all;

we dedicate this house.

In gratitude for the labors of all who love and serve this church; in loving remembrance of those who have finished their course; in the hope of eternal life through Jesus Christ our Lord;

we dedicate this house.

CLOSING PRAYER

We now, the people of this church, surrounded by a great cloud of witnesses, grateful for our heritage, aware of the sacrifices of our mothers and fathers in the faith, and confessing that apart from us their work cannot be made perfect, do dedicate ourselves anew to the worship and service of Almighty God; through Jesus Christ our Lord. **Amen.**

HYMN

BLESSING

An Order for the Consecration of an Educational Building

This *order* is designed to be a service of worship in itself. It may be used for the opening and consecration of an educational or education-administration building of a local church or school. For an order to be used celebrating the payment of the indebtedness on such a building, see page 50.

SCRIPTURE SENTENCES

Blessed be the name of God for ever and ever,
to whom belong wisdom and might.
God gives wisdom to the wise
and knowledge to those who have understanding.

HYMN OF PRAISE

DECLARATION OF PURPOSE

Dear friends, this building, which by the favor of God and human labor has been so far completed, embodies the obligation of each generation to impart its treasures of wisdom and knowledge to the generation following. For the fulfillment of this task we need, not only the best that we can do, but above all the blessing of Almighty God. Let us, therefore, bring praise to God for his aid in this undertaking, giving thanks for those who by their gifts of their service shall unite in fulfilling the purpose for which this building is prepared.

SCRIPTURE LESSON—*Proverbs 3:13-19*

ACT OF PRAISE—*Psalms 119:1-16 or an Anthem*

SCRIPTURE LESSON—*Philippians 2:1-11*

HYMN

GOSPEL LESSON—*John 14:15-17, 25-26; 16:12-13*

SERMON

OFFERING

HYMN OR ANTHEM

PRESENTATION OF THE BUILDING

Members of the Board of Trustees or of another appropriate committee stand before the minister, and an appointed member says:

We present this building to be consecrated to the glory of Almighty God and for service in the enlightenment of God's people.

If the building is to be a memorial, the phrase is added:
in loving memory of *(Name)*.

ACT OF CONSECRATION

Dear friends, it is with joy that we gather to consecrate this building. But the consecration of this building is vain without the consecration of those whose gifts it represents. Let us give ourselves anew to the service of God: our minds, that they may be renewed after the image of Christ; our bodies, they they may be fit temples for the indwelling of the Holy Spirit; and our labors, that they may be according to God's will, and that their fruit may glorify God's name and serve God's eternal purposes.

In the name of the Father, and of the Son, and of the Holy Spirit,

we consecrate this building.

To the spiritual enrichment of all who shall come here seeking knowledge,

we consecrate this building.

To the loyal service of those whose training and devotion have prepared them to lead students toward the truth,

we consecrate this building.

To that ministry of administration upon whose ability and fruitfulness depends the wise conduct of our life together and our ministry in the world, we consecrate this building; and we consecrate ourselves anew to that service of humanity in which we perform the true service of God.

CLOSING PRAYER

Let us pray.
Almighty God, hear us who gather here to consecrate ourselves to your service. Grant that those who come here, whether as administrators, teachers, or students, may come with inquiring minds, honest purpose, and steadfast endeavor to do your holy will. We give thanks to you for all your servants, our parents, teachers, benefactors, and friends, by whose love and devotion we have come into our great inheritance of health, truth, and faith. Help us guard this treasure, be blessed by it, nurture it, and pass it on to the coming generation, that they may serve you; in the name of Jesus Christ our Lord. **Amen.**

HYMN

BLESSING

An Order for the Consecration of a Hospital

SCRIPTURE SENTENCES

Our help is in the name of the Lord
who made heaven and earth.
O give thanks to the Lord, for he is good
for his steadfast love endures forever.

HYMN OF PRAISE

DECLARATION OF PURPOSE

Dear friends, this building, which by the favor of God and human labor has been so far completed, is a symbol of that care for the sick and suffering exemplified in our Lord Jesus Christ, which has always inspired those who follow him. We believe that God desires and accepts the service of comfort and healing which this building will make possible, because with a motherly compassion God loves all of earth's children. Let us, therefore, bring our praises and ask for guidance and help in this adventure. Let us give thanks for those who by their gifts and services shall unite in fulfilling the purposes of love and skill for which this building is prepared.

SCRIPTURE LESSON—*Isaiah 61:1-2a; 35:3-6a*

ACT OF PRAISE—*Psalm 103:1-4, 13-18, 20-22, or an Anthem*

SCRIPTURE LESSON—*Acts 3:1-10*

HYMN

GOSPEL LESSON—*Luke 7:18-23*

SERMON

OFFERING

HYMN OR ANTHEM

PRESENTATION OF THE BUILDING
Members of the Board of Trustees or of another appropriate committee stand before the people, and an appointed member says to the presider:

We present this building to be consecrated to the glory of Almighty God and for service in the relief of the sick and the suffering.

If the building is to be a memorial, the phrase is added:
In loving memory of *(Name)*.

ACT OF CONSECRATION
Dear friends, it is with joy that we gather to consecrate this building. But the consecration of this building is in vain

without the consecration of those whose gifts it represents. Let us give ourselves anew to the service of God: our minds, that they may be renewed after the image of Christ; our bodies, that they may be fit temples for the indwelling of the Holy Spirit; and our labors, that they may be according to God's will, and that their fruit may glorify God's name and serve God's eternal purposes.

In the name of the Father, and of the Son, and of the Holy Spirit,

we consecrate this building.

To the holy ministry of healing, and the sustaining power of the Holy Spirit in time of pain and suffering,

we consecrate this building.

To the skill and wisdom that bring relief and cure, and to the patient research that uncovers fresh resources with which to serve the public health,

we consecrate this building; and we consecrate ourselves anew to that service of humanity in which we perform the true service of God.

CLOSING PRAYER

Let us pray.
Almighty God, hear us who gather here to dedicate ourselves to your service. Let this building, consecrated to your service and glory, be a place where skill and tenderness may unite to bring health and cure to those who come for aid. May those who come here in weakness be made strong; may those who come in pain find relief, and those who come in sorrow find joy and happiness; through Jesus Christ our Lord. **Amen.**

HYMN

BLESSING

An Order for the Consecration of a Dwelling

SCRIPTURE SENTENCE

"Behold, I stand at the door and knock;
if any one hears my voice and opens the door,
I will come in" (Revelation 3:20).

DECLARATION OF PURPOSE

Dear friends, we have gathered here to seek God's blessing upon this house, which by the favor of God and human labor has been so far completed. A house is not only our dwelling but a symbol to us of God's loving care and of our life together as the family of Christ. Let us therefore bring praise and thanksgiving for goodness and mercy and for our communion, offering ourselves as God's servants and as loving sisters and brothers to one another.

OPENING PRAYER

Let us pray.
Eternal God, you govern all things in heaven and earth, and make all things new through your almighty Word. We thank you for your faithfulness and bless your holy name. Shed your rays of light upon this household that *those* who live here may be confident of your guidance and walk with steady faith. Be close in time of stress or pain and give courage and hope that never fails; through Jesus Christ our Lord. **Amen.**

SCRIPTURE LESSON—*I John 4:11-21 or Ephesians 3:14-21*

ACT OF CONSECRATION

In the name of the Father, and of the Son, and of the Holy Spirit, we consecrate this home, committing to God's love and care this house and *all* who dwell therein. **Amen.**

CLOSING PRAYER

Let us pray.

Eternal God, bless this home. Let your love rest upon it and your promised presence be manifested in it. May *(the members of this household, Name)* grow in grace and in the knowledge of our Lord Jesus Christ. Teach *them* to love, as you have given us commandment; and help us all to live in the peace of Jesus Christ our Lord. **Amen.**

The service may conclude here with the Lord's Prayer and blessing, or it may continue as indicated below.

SYMBOLIC ACTS

At this point symbolic expressions may be appropriate: the presentation of a gift such as a painting or other work, or the planting of a tree or shrub. These actions could be accompanied by suitable blessings.

HOLY COMMUNION

It is appropriate to gather the people for a household celebration of Holy Communion, administered by an authorized minister, using the dining table as the Lord's table and perhaps bread baked in the oven of the new home. The minister takes the bread and cup, prepares the bread and wine for the meal, and then prays the Great Thanksgiving as follows:

Lift up your heart(s) and give thanks to the Lord our God.

Father Almighty, Creator of heaven and earth, you made us in your image, to love and to be loved. When we turned away, and our love failed, your love remained steadfast.

By the suffering, death, and resurrection of your only Son Jesus Christ you delivered us from slavery to sin and death and made with us a new covenant by water and the Spirit.

On the night in which he gave himself up for us he took bread, gave thanks to you, broke the bread, gave it to his disciples, and said: "Take, eat; this is my body which is given for you. Do this in remembrance of me."

When supper was over he took the cup, gave thanks to you, gave it to his disciples, and said: "Drink from this, all of you;

this is my blood of the new covenant, poured out for you and for many for the forgiveness of sins. Do this, as often as you drink it, in remembrance of me."

And so, in remembrance of these your mighty acts in Jesus Christ, we offer ourselves in praise and thanksgiving as a holy and living sacrifice, in union with Christ's offering for us.

Pour out your Holy Spirit on us and on these gifts of bread and wine. Make them be for us the body and blood of Christ, that we may be for the world the body of Christ, redeemed by his blood. By your Spirit make us one with Christ, one with each other, and one in ministry to all the world, until Christ comes in final victory and we feast at his heavenly banquet.

Through your Son Jesus Christ, with the Holy Spirit in your holy church, all honor and glory is yours, Almighty Father, now and forever. **Amen.**

And now, with the confidence of children of God, let us pray.

All pray the Lord's Prayer.

The minister breaks the bread.

The bread and wine are given to the people, with these or other words being exchanged:

The body of Christ, given for you. **Amen.**
The blood of Christ, given for you. **Amen.**

When all have received, the table is put in order. The minister may then give thanks after Communion.

BLESSING
"The Lord bless you and keep you.
  The Lord make his face to shine upon you,
    and be gracious unto you.
  The Lord lift up his countenance upon you,
    and give you peace" (Numbers 6:24-26). **Amen.**

An Order for the Consecration of Church Furnishings and Memorials

This *order* is intended to be used within a service of worship. When used separately, it should follow appropriate prayer and praise, Scripture lessons, and sermon.

The donor, or someone designated to present the gift or memorial, stands before the minister and says:
We present this *(gift, memorial)* to be consecrated to the glory of Almighty God and for service in this church.

If the gift is to be a memorial, the phrase is added:
in loving memory of *(Name)*.

Other phrases may also be added as appropriate.

The person designated to accept the gift says:
We accept this gift as a sacred trust and will guard and use it reverently.

If the gift is to be a memorial, the phrase is added:
in honor of the faithful and devoted life in whose memory it is given.

Other phrases may also be added as appropriate.

Then the minister says:
In the name of the Father, and of the Son, and of the Holy Spirit, we consecrate this *(gift, memorial)* to the glory of God.

If the gift is to be a memorial, the phrase is added:
and in memory of the servant of the Lord *(Name)*. The memory of the righteous is ever blessed.

Other phrases may also be added as appropriate.

May those who love your salvation say continually, "Great is the Lord."

Yea, our hearts are glad
because we trust in the holy name.

Let us make a joyful noise with songs of praise.

We praise you, O God;
we acknowledge you to be the Lord.

Let us pray.
Most loving God, without you no words or works of ours
have meaning. Accept the gifts of our hands as symbols of
our devotion. Grant us your blessing, as we consecrate this
gift to your glory, that it may be an enduring witness before
all your people, and that our lives may be consecrated in your
service; through Jesus Christ our Lord. **Amen.**

*If the service concludes here, a hymn may be sung and a blessing
given.*

An Order for the Dedication
of an Organ or
Other Musical Instruments

This *order* is intended to be used within a service of
worship. When used separately, it should follow appropriate
prayer and praise, Scripture lessons, and sermon.

*The donor, or someone designated to present the instrument, stands
before the minister and says:*
We present this *organ* to be consecrated to the glory of
Almighty God and for service in this church.

If the instrument is to be a memorial, the phrase is added:
in loving memory of *(Name).*

The minister and people respond:
It is good to give thanks to the Lord.
to sing praises to your name, O Most High,
to declare your steadfast love in the morning,
and your faithfulness at night,

to the music of the lute and the harp.
to the melody of the lyre.
For you, O Lord, have made me glad by your work;
at the works of your hands I sing for joy.

Then all shall sing the Gloria Patri *or some other doxological stanza.*

Here dedicatory music is played on the instrument or instruments to be consecrated.

Then the minister says:
Let us pray.
Eternal God, whom the generations have worshiped through the gift of music, accept our praise to you in the sound of this instrument, which we consecrate in your name and to your glory. Grant that its music may be a blessing to all who worship here, and that they may be consecrated to you, whose sound has gone out through all the earth and whose words to the end of the world. Let our music be so joined to your holy Word that your glory may surround us and empower us for the service to which you call us in the world, through Jesus Christ our Lord. **Amen.**

If the service concludes here, a hymn may be sung and a blessing given.